650 | At The Bar

Edited by Edward McCann

650 | WHERE WRITERS READ

Founder / Editor • Edward Mccann
Executive Producer • Richard Kollath
Literary Ombudsman & Senior Editor • Steven Lewis
Director of Operations • Jane Kaupp
Design Director • Diane Fokas
Social Media Strategist • Shayna Miller
Director of Photography • Kevin O'Connor
Chief Audio Engineer • Jesse Chason
Videography / Photography • Sara Caldwell
Copy Editor • Shelley Sadler Kenney
Technical Advisor • Conrad Trautmann
Technical Advisor • Stephen Kaupp

Production Assistants
Robert Dennison, Lynn Dennison, Mackenzie Meeks,
Jackie Mercurio, Brian Reagher, and Isabella Fokas

Advisory Committee
Rachel Aydt, Laura Shaine Cunningham, Angela Davis-Gardner, Karen
Dukess, Joseph Goodrich, David Masello, Honor Molloy, Irene O'Garden,
John Pielmeier, Gretchen Reed, James Russek,
Angela Derecas Taylor and Julie Trelstad

"I like bars just after they open for the evening. When the air inside is still cool and clean and everything is shiny and the barkeep is giving himself that last look in the mirror to see if his tie is straight and his hair is smooth."

-- *Raymond Chandler*

ABOUT 650

So – the Bar. Or the pub, or tavern, or saloon, or lounge, or canteen. You'll find them all over the world in nearly every culture, and you might even know of one in your aunt and uncle's finished basement. It's a social spot, a watering hole, a dating and mating market, and a port in a storm. And whether it's *Cheers* or the *Bada Bing*, every bar everywhere is a launching point for stories. For this volume, we've collected a dozen stories about bars written by a dozen very talented writers—work that reflects a range of perspectives and experiences.

650 is a celebration of writing and the spoken word, a literary forum for personal stories performed five minutes—and 650 words—at a time. Our events at theaters, colleges, and libraries around the country are organized around single, broad topics that invite a range of expression, and recorded performances are added to a digital archive of writers reading their work aloud. The writers and their work receive additional exposure through podcasts, broadcasts, our YouTube channel, and in these printed volumes. The volume you hold in your hands is a collection of stories featured at a sold-out event at Nancy Manocherian's *the cell* in New York City.

650 features graduate students and grandparents, first-timers and best-selleing writers. It's all about the writing, with an emphasis on craft. It's about the choice of one word over another, about the shape of sentences and paragraphs, the arc of a narrative, the poetry of a unique literary voice. If you love language and enjoy a good story, you've come to the right place. To submit your work or attend our shows, visit our website or Facebook page, and join our mailing list.

Please tell your friends about 650, and spread the word about the spoken word.

Ed McCann

Edward McCann, Founder / Editor

READ650.COM
FACEBOOK.COM/READ650

CONTENTS

650 | At The Bar

Edited by Edward McCann

JESSICA RAO

Jessica Rao has done just about every kind of writing there is. She has been an award-winning business contributor at CNBC.com and a lifestyle writer for Gannett. She's written magazine articles, blog posts, and three school books published by McGraw Hill. She taught writing to high school students and has run her own PR firm. These days, as a mom of two, Jessica needs a few more hours on any given day, and she blogs about it at *TimeInsensitive*. Jessica is also a student at the Writing Institute at Sarah Lawrence College, where she has recently completed a novel about a nineteen-year-old Brooklyn girl who drops out of school to become a waitress.

NO PROOF

Jessica Rao

As a teenager living in Brooklyn in the eighties, it wasn't hard to buy beer. Getting in to a bar was a different story. You had to know which ones wouldn't card you. But somehow, we figured it out, and by the time I graduated high school, I'd shot pool at the Alibi Club, my neighborhood dive, listened to a long-haired-dude sing Miss American Pie at the Back Fence on Bleeker Street, and drank Budweiser from plastic pitchers in a dark room called the Speakeasy around the corner on MacDougal.

When I went to college in Albany, New York, however, the bar game changed. There were no old men willing to look the other way while kids bounced quarters off tables into pint glasses. The college bars had big football players propped up outside and you needed good fake ID to get in. That, or you or one of your friends had to be doing it with (or on the verge of doing it with) the bartender, bouncer, or singer in the band. In that case, you could get in with your cafeteria meal card.

There was no place for the laminated plastic card I bought in Times Square a couple of years before. My friend and I put on a lot of make up, took the A train to 42nd, and within a couple of blocks found a smoke shop

1

offering Marlboros, triple X videos, and ID Cards. We got our pictures taken and when we left we were twenty-one.

The best way to get a fake ID was to have your older sister (or brother) give you their license. The second was to have your license "chalked," like turn a '72 into a '69. Last, was how I got mine: find someone who made out-of-state licenses. I paid the friend of a friend two hundred dollars for a fake "Florida." There was a little talked-about fourth way, but I only knew a couple of people who did it. Get a fake birth certificate and go to the DMV and get a real, fake non-drivers ID.

My friend Rebecca was ahead of the curve. She came to college with a fake "Jersey." One night, she and I and two friends got into a bar called Holidays. It was pre-Florida and we used another less popular tactic—the passback—which involved four girls and two IDs. We drank beer and pink shots and watched ourselves dance in the mirror, as a strobe light flicked on and off.

Later, while I danced with a guy named Jimbo, the music stopped and a voice said, "Heather Vance. Come to the bar. We have your license." I looked around for Heather, aka Rebecca, but I didn't see her. My stomach turned over. I left Jimbo and found Rebecca standing with our friends. "They just paged Heather Vance! Didn't you hear? They have your license!"

"Oh my god. Should I go get it? What if we get busted?"

We decided that we had to try and the four of us filed through the bar.

"I'm Heather Vance," Rebecca said to a bartender with slicked back hair.

"You're the Jersey girls?"

I gulped. "Born and raised."

He walked away and came back with another guy. He looked at Rebecca and then down at the license. He turned it over and held it up to his face. "Alright," he said, "I forgive you, being from Jersey and all."

Years later, I was at the hair salon getting a blowout. The young woman washing my hair asked, "Any special plans tonight?"

"My husband and I are going out with friends. What about you?"

"Probably going to the bars on Mamaroneck Ave," she said, drying her hands to check her phone.

"Sounds fun."

"Yeah, sort of. But now that I'm 21, it's not as fun as it used to be—everyone is young."

TOM NOLAN

Writer and photographer **Tom Nolan** lives in New Paltz, New York with his wife Carol. His writing has appeared in literary Journals and *Fictionique,* an online repository for short fiction. Tom's blog, *Musings from the Gunks,* refers to the Shawangunk Ridge near his Hudson Valley home. A collection of Tom's short stories, *Wishbone Creek and Other Stories* is available from Amazon, as is *Second Cutting,* his first novel.

THE EMPIRE HOUSE

Tom Nolan

I grew up in Gilbertsville, New York, an odd little village nestled in the Butternut Valley of Otsego County. When my family arrived in the early fifties, it had three churches (Episcopal, Presbyterian, and Baptist), three gas stations (Esso, Shell, and Sinclair), and one bar. Locals referred to it as The Ho'tel. The reason for the emphasis on the first syllable is lost to history. One reached it via a gravel path through the garden on the east side of the Empire House, a one-time hotel that had been converted into apartments and a restaurant. Eddie, a compact, powerfully built Scot, ran the place with his wife, Hilda, and entertained his clientele with stories of his exploits as a paratrooper in World War II.

When he told of dropping behind German lines to blow up bridges or railroad trestles and then finding his way back with the help of resistance fighters, we were glued to the tales, though we heard more than a few variations of them throughout our high school years. Whether true or not, the telling, in his faint brogue with his wooly-bear eyebrows raised and eyes wide as he explained his escape, was great entertainment. If it wasn't busy, he'd challenge one of us to arm wrestle—his elbow on the bar, Popeye-sized forearm vertical, hand open, ready to engage. He always won. Whenever he poured a can of beer, he'd crush the steel can in his fist before tossing it in the trash; if he poured a bottle, he'd bend the steel cap between thumb and forefinger.

The only people in the small room immune to Eddie's war stories and feats of strength were Walt and Art; Walt, in a dark blue T-shirt and bib overalls, his right shoulder against the wall, left foot on the rail; Art in a once-white shirt, tails hanging out of his khaki trousers, mirrored Walt's stance at the other end of the mahogany bar. Each had his hand around a mug of beer, which Eddie refreshed at regular intervals. Each communed with his reflection in the bar mirror. Neither acknowledged the other's presence, nor that of anyone else, though they lifted their mugs and drank in unison. Eddie said they were always at the door when he opened at noon, and left together at midnight.

The three walls not occupied by shelves of alcohol and the mirror contained a mural by the talented son of Frank and Helen, the owners of Empire House. It rendered the inside of the room; the booths against the far wall were shown above the actual booths, and as one looked from side to side, Art and Walt were leaning on the wall just below their likenesses. When I asked Eddie how long ago it was painted, he thought a bit then answered, "Fourteen years past."

On May 15, 1959, several members of the high school baseball team burst in raucously reliving a win. Leading the pack, I caused a comic accordion collision of the eight behind me as I stopped. Walt and Art weren't there. Eddie explained that when he unlocked the place only Walt appeared.

Walking to his spot, he downed the beer waiting for him, then moved to Art's place and drank that one. Without a word he put a fifty on the bar and left. That information held us teens silent for only a few seconds before we resumed our celebration.

A decade later, I returned to the village and the Ho'tel. Eddie's hair and brows were gray but his physique had not changed. Over mugs of Genesee Cream Ale, we caught each other up. When I asked about Walt and Art, he told me that day was the last anyone saw of either man. Yes, we arm wrestled. Yes, he won.

LYNN BEVILLE

Lynn Beville is a lifelong resident of Westchester County, New York, where she worked as a social worker in schools and in child care for over thirty years. She often used visual, literary and performing arts in her work with children and adolescents, finding these arts helped kids express themselves more adequately than other therapies. She has been a writer and performer of poetry since the 1980s and a veteran of community theatre and vocal workshop performances in Harlem, Midtown and Greenwich Village in Manhattan. Lynn also does freelance writing for *Harlem Times*, an on-line and traditionally published newspaper. Mentored by Steven Lewis, writer and instructor at the Writing Institute at Sarah Lawrence College, Lynn has been published in two independent collections of microfiction produced by Mr. Lewis.

McSORLEY'S ALE TALE

Lynn Beville

The Tudor facade made the bar stand out on an otherwise non-descript side street in Westchester, a borderline between a commercial district and a rather upscale neighborhood a few blocks away. Patrons lived mostly in the borderline neighborhood. They liked to drink boilermakers, a combination of whiskey chased by ale. It was a rather anonymous existence so I had to imagine that was what the nondescript patrons wanted.

A mysterious but charming and urbane man I was seeing liked to relax there and drink the ale. One evening, he stood deep in the rear of the second room, staring at the jukebox selections. The room was dark and adjacent to the bar where I sat waiting, wondering how long I'd have to endure the hapless culture that the regulars seemed to relish. It haunted me to know someone I lived with also sought the dim refuge there.

He was clad in navy blue slacks and a golf jacket. He had a slightly bent posture, one hand in the pocket of his slacks, looking like a model waiting to be captured for a *GQ* collegiate page spread.

I sat there thinking back and forth between my *GQ* man and a young coquette who lived with her boyfriend down the hall from us in the same English Tudor apartment building. In these few private moments, I understood that she would soon devastate her boyfriend and seduce mine.

I had already confirmed the signs. One evening when I turned the key to the door coming home from work, I found her in our apartment, curled up, dozing in a yellow skirt and sweater. Also when the four of us were together, her man had the pathetic cuckold look in his countenance.

Standing in the tavern, bathing in the last vestiges of possession, I breathed in my own sweet memories and walked up to him. "Hi ... I'm here." I uttered softly. He and I joined hands, walking to the bar. "McSorley's Ale" he called out. Then he gazed at me with affection. "What'll you have?" We sat talking in the ways we had in so many carefree times. He guzzled the sour amber-foamed stuff as I sipped, lady-like, on a gin and tonic.

A short time later, the coquette came in and took a stool nearby. We said hello and returned to our conversation. We seemed to have much to talk about, laughing at private jokes, moving through our rendezvous without notice of how our neighbor's eyes were closing in. She'd been downing boiler makers in uninterrupted sequence.

Suddenly, in what seemed like slow motion, she listed and fell off the bar stool landing with a splat on the floor. She uttered no sound in the fall ... or as she landed. She just lay there stunned ... eyes still half mast. Several gallant but nondescript drinkers leapt to her aid, including my knight in navy blue.

The beginning of my end.

AT THE BAR

ANN LEVIN

Ann Levin is a freelance writer and editor in New York City. She worked for The Associated Press (AP) for twenty years as a reporter and editor, most of the time based in Manhattan. Before that, she reported for papers in Texas and San Diego. Since leaving the AP in 2009, she has worked as an editor for the United Nations Population Fund and Columbia University, written articles for the *AARP Bulletin* and other publications, and contributed book reviews to the AP. She lives on New York City's Upper East Side with her husband, Stan Honda, a photographer.

IN VINO VERITAS

Ann Levin

The first time I got drunk I danced a jig in the middle of my aunt and uncle's living room while my mother, father, and brothers and sisters looked on. I was eight years old, and my dad had given me a teaspoonful of red wine at a holiday dinner. It was too long ago to remember how I felt, but someone snapped a picture so I know how I looked. I had on a black-and-white polka dot dress with pleats, white ankle socks and black patent leather shoes—and from my flushed cheeks and mischievous grin, you can tell I was one deliriously happy girl.

The Latin phrase, "in vino veritas," translates to "in wine, there is truth," and sometimes it seems that way. Fast forward fifteen years.

Now I'm sitting in a dark neighborhood bar in the Fenway section of Boston with my boyfriend at the time. The jukebox is playing, and we get up to dance. Midway through the song, an old barfly we'd been talking to hoisted himself up off his bar stool to go to the bathroom. On the way he grabbed my friend's arm, leaned in and slurred in a beery Boston brogue, "You should marry this woman. She listens." For years afterward, I

13

thought of myself as "the woman who listens." Was that old drunk right? Yes and no. Sometimes I listen, and sometimes I don't.

That relationship didn't last more than a few years—although in another sweet, drunken moment, I did propose to him. That time we were drinking in a country saloon off a rural road in central Texas. As the alcohol began its pleasant work of numbing my brain, I glanced at the sawdust on the wood plank floor, the rough, gray wood of the walls, the swinging doors like the ones in the movies, and I said, "Let's get married! Let's get married here!" Wisely, he said no. He must have known I was more in love with the décor than with him. In vino veritas? In that case, no.

Here's the tricky thing about alcohol: It delivers suggestions to the brain that seem like very good ideas at the time. But within hours or weeks or months or sometimes years, those brilliant notions turn out to have been impractical, foolish or wrong. And yet every now and then—and this is what makes it hard—I discover there is truth in wine. And in the mixture of alcohol and pills.

A few years after I graduated from college, I went out dancing with a friend. It was the late 1970s, and disco was still the rage. She liked to mix wine and Valium, and following her lead, I acquired my own supply. That night was the first time I had ever taken the two of them together. Even now, decades later, I can still remember how it felt. I wasn't light-headed or tipsy, and I didn't feel bloated or sick, as I sometimes do when I'm drinking. No, I was focused and alert, aware of my body but free of its fleshy burden. I felt confident, capable, satisfied and sexy. In love with the world and supremely glad to be alive.

It was a sensation that—as young and reckless, stoned and drunk, as I was—I somehow knew was too good to be true.

What did I do? I marched off the dance floor to the women's bathroom, entered a stall, fumbled around for the vial of Valium in my pocket, pried off the lid, and flushed the contents down the toilet. I can still see the water swirling in the bowl, washing those tiny pills into the Boston sewer system.

HONOR MOLLOY

Honor Molloy is a playwright and the author of the autobiographical novel *Smarty Girl—Dublin Savage*, a fictionalized version of her childhood in Ireland. Her play *Crackskull Row* (New York Times Critics' Pick) was developed and produced by Nancy Manocherian's the cell. This world premiere won best production and best direction (Kira Simring) awards as part of Origin's First Irish Theatre Festival 2016. The Irish Repertory Theatre subsequently moved the cell's production to their W. Scott McLucas Studio Theatre for a seven-week run. An alumna of New Dramatists, Molloy has received support from the National Endowment for the Arts and the New York Foundation for the Arts, and was awarded a fellowship year at the Radcliffe Institute for Advanced Study at Harvard.

103

Honor Molloy

Three thirty three a.m. East Village. It's 1984, Mister Bowie. Never imagined they'd reach it. Thought the world would blow.

She's working the cash register, mind on the tide of color and sound. Only there 'cause. This afternoon. Lorna called. Left a message on her answering machine. Can she cover for Rodge? He has a cold. Graveyard shift. Graveyard? These kids are alive.

Crowd's a throbbing thing, six deep at the bar. Jukebox throwing triangles of orange, violet, lime on their faces like celluloid. Jukebox. Tossing out Patsy. She's walking after midnight. They are serving after midnight. Cater to pseudos, the hip and the hep, spillovers from The Saint. Emancipation nation just next door. Damp from dancing, poppers, all-night-sex—come dawn, men wobble out, drop to the pavement. Ambulance sweeps in, whips them away.

That graffiti artist in blue Armani, splattered in paint. Quentin Crisp in the lavender shirt, matching lavender coif, holding court in the window.

Overlooking Second Ave.

Stiffed me. Izzy's chasing a small guy out the door. You're 86'ed. Hurls a tin disk. Bounces off Small Guy's back. Gimme my four bucks, *schah-muck*. And Izzy's after him. Running 'gainst the light.

She grabs Small Guy's tip off the floor. A pin. Pale blue. With a deep purple radioactive man. Clips it to the waist of her 501s. Place is noisy with regulars: Art junkies, heart junkies, junkie-junkies. Come to worship in the black-tiled mens room. Set their works on shelves of bright stainless steel.

Not everyone's on shift tonight, but here's her faves: Tronno Raj, modern dancer. Before Martha Graham, he did ballet; host for the night— Alphonso the butch-queen; Lorna-the-actor, from North Caroliniahhh. Accent thick as a slabba ham.

Over there at her station, Risa. Sneaking a Gitane. One. Long. Last. Pull-on-her-smoke before plunging it into a plate a steak so rare, bloody as a stigmatist.

And Geranium. Rockabilly hair, run through with oil. Heel of her top boot hooked to the barstool's rung. Bored to extinction, sipping her third green Pernod. Black eyes, black-black-black, slice the room. Alight on Girl, slight as a boy. In a tutu of charcoal tulle. Under her matador jacket, Girl is bare. No bra, no tee, no. Nothing.

Bum a cig? Girl says.

Geranium laughs. A husky bark. Already fishing for Dunhill Red. 'Hind the cash register, She thinks. This is gonna fall. Fall Crazy. But cannot look away.

Geranium's hands wrap Girl's waistband. Runs a thumb from navel to sternum. Tips the flap of Girl's matador coat, takes a peek. Geranium.

Glances at Girl with scorn.

She stands. A full six feet one. Her eyes, black-black-black, her. Eyes slide aside. She's done. Slaps a fifty on the counter. She's gone.

Left in the rough, Girl smiles. Eyes starry with tears. Swoops up Geranium's change. Orders a house white. Side a homefries. With skin.

The next day. Next day. Lorna calls, voice dulled since yesterday. States it fast, states it quick: Raj. Went from a cough to can't-catch-his-breath. Some gunk in his lungs. To St. Vincent's to complete respiratory failure within four hours. Once he hit the hospital sheets, never opened his eyes. Again.

There on his sick bed. Sweat slimes his temples. His chest. He's white to the teeth. Respirator sucking him up off the bed, through the tubes, in to the machine.

Falling-falling. He keeps falling. Reach up. Reach up.

Respirator. Forcing oxygen in. Raj jerks and flicks. The pull-and-hiss. Hiss-and-pull. Until. Flat line. All goes still. Far from Toronto, the boy slips out of the quiet room. Into another land.

Lorna's phone call sends a ribbon of terror along her nerves. Mouth fills with spit, she vomits.

Once, of an emptied afternoon, in the changing of shifts, Raj danced for her. On the hardwood runway mid the vacant chairs, he bounds tabletop to tabletop. From table to bar. Then leaps. A grand jete. Petite plie. Raj dips his head and bows.

STEVEN LEWIS

Steven Lewis, Literary Ombudsman for 650, is a columnist at *Talking Writing*, and a member of the Sarah Lawrence College Writing Institute faculty. A longtime freelancer, his work has been published in *The New York Times, The Washington Post, Christian Science Monitor, the Los Angeles Times, Ploughshares, Spirituality & Health* and others. Recent novels include *Take This, Loving Violet,* and *A Hard Rain,* all from Codhill Press, and Finishing Line Press published Steve's poetry chapbook, *If I Die Before You Wake.* His backlist includes *Zen and the Art of Fatherhood, The ABCs of Real Family Values, The Complete Guide for the Anxious Groom,* and *Fear and Loathing of Boca Raton (a Hippie's Guide to the New Sixties).* He divides his time between his writing space in New Paltz, New York and Hatteras Island, North Carolina.

THE BARD AT THE BAR

Steven Lewis

My freshman roommate at the University of Wisconsin, perhaps sensing that I had scuttled my way through high school by copying Judy Goldstein's papers, informs me that to save my silly suburbanized soul I should write poetry. I shrug. He's clearly an idiot. I follow my cool new friends to The Pub on State Street.

Six weeks later, Judy-less, clueless, dateless, depressed, and a pitcher-inebriated at the beer joint, I recall Dan Depperman's prescription for my soul and find a napkin, borrow a grimy pencil from the bartender, and begin to scribble a self-absorbed, whiney, pathetic woe-is-me ode to loneliness.

Midway into my final hand-wringing rhymed couplet, a slinky girl dressed in black comes over, puts her slinky white hand on my hunched shoulder and asks what I'm doing. I instantly recognize her as one of a dozen girls with long black hair, black eyeliner, black turtlenecks, black skirts, black tights, and black Pappagallos who refused to dance—or talk—with me an hour before.

So when I tell her, somewhat sheepishly (after all, I'm writing a poem on the advice of an idiot), she doesn't turn away without changing expression, like she did when I asked her to dance. She asks what it's about.

I don't tell her it's about my deplorable social life. Or the Ds on all my six-week tests. Or my burgeoning understanding that I am not the most special Long Island Jew that Madison has even seen. And while I have not actually read Camus's The Myth of Sisyphus, I did wake up momentarily in my 8 a.m. freshman comp class and heard someone say something about futility and the meaninglessness of life. So I nod and say very somberly, "The meaninglessness of life." And when her head tilts and a sympathetic smile forms on her thin lips, I add, "Futility."

And thus I nab my first college date.

A few nights later, rather than do the reading for Meteorology (a five-credit class in which I am destined to get a D minus (and later explain to my outraged parents "You don't need a weatherman to know which way the wind blows"), I return to The Pub, write another bad poem about despair, which I title "Futility 2," and another wan creature in black slinks over and wants to know what I'm doing: Date #2.

In the weeks that follow, I write more terrible poems and attract more cute slinky girls who seem to like me for no other reason than I write poems about wretchedness. So does my twenty-two year old Freshman Comp TA after I show her "Futility 14."

By second semester, now solidly on academic probation, I write more dreadful poems on dirty napkins in coffee houses and pubs around Madison … and meet more beatnik girls who like to save miserable boys who will flunk out if they don't get a 2.0 GPA.

The following fall I arrive back in Madison with a rounded up 2.0 GPA, a scraggly goatee, enough curly hair to fill most doorways, and reams of shamelessly shameful poetry in a red rope folder.

First stop is The Pub where I look around to scout out the best writing location, and see sallow boys dressed in black all over the dark bar, a bevy of my Joan Baez lookalikes at their elbows. Instantly bereft, I find a corner and scribble a poorly constructed, self-absorbed, whiny, pathetic woe-is-me poem about—what else?—not being noticed.

No one notices.

I title it "I Am Invisible 1."

BRENDAN COSTELLO JR.

Brendan Costello Jr. teaches creative writing at The City College of New York, where he earned his MFA. His fiction and non-fiction have appeared in *Salon.com, Open Letters Monthly, smokebox.net,* and *Epiphany* magazine. He is also the former producer and co-host of *The Largest Minority* on WBAI radio in New York, was a contributing editor of *Lurch* magazine and is on the board of the Irish-American Writers & Artists.

LAST CALL AT FREDDY'S

Brendan Costello

The end for Freddy's Bar was a long time coming, with a couple of false alarms and a few fleeting false hopes. It had been rated "best bar" in Brooklyn, in New York City, and one of the best bars in America by various publications, but the most important accolade was its designation as home for its regulars, a mix of old-timers, artists, hipsters and genuine people of all stripes. Located at the border of Park Slope and Prospect Heights, Freddy's had a backroom featuring free live music, an in-house literary magazine, and a series of artfully disturbing video mashups, created by head bartender Donald O'Finn, constantly playing on the TV.

Unfortunately, it fell in the footprint of the Atlantic Yards project, and thanks to eminent domain, greedy developers, and politicians acting in the public's worst interest, Freddy's was slated for demolition. It became home to the resistance—Develop Don't Destroy Brooklyn.

Good fight fought, options exhausted, it came time for the official final blowout. Regulars, old friends, new friends, hipsters and hopsters all descended on the place like alcoholic locusts. The bar overflowed and the scene outside was as crazy as it was packed inside. Singing, shouting, quiet remembrances of friends long gone and hilarious recountings of our misadventures spilled out over neon-tinted sidewalks.

Chaos and lunacy reigned within. The place was filled beyond capacity, and no one wanted to leave, even when Blue the bartender did her precarious fire dance on top of the bar. I didn't even make it inside until four o'clock in the morning when they chased out all but the most loyal regulars. Our mission was a familiar one: drink until we were unrecognizable, and the place was uninhabitable.

Despite losing the bar, we did not despair. We knew the spirit of the place would live on. Rather than feeling like we were on a sinking ship, it felt like we were taking flight—even as the ship was coming apart. The stuffed marlin, the moosehead, and the human skeleton were already gone (in safekeeping), and partiers took whatever mementos they could pry from the walls, tables and floors.

During the busy part of the evening, folks threw money at the bartenders, to help sustain them between jobs and to aid in the relocation effort. Now, though, money was no longer even a question—we laughed at the ancient cash registers. Now it was just about finishing the booze that was still here.

At one point, bartender and DJ Ben opened a forgotten cubby behind the bar and discovered an unopened bottle of Jameson Gold—was this the giving tree of bars? Here we were, switching to the good stuff at five o'clock in the morning—like a story out of the damn bible!

Around sunrise Donald, our unofficial patriarch, threw his glass against the wall, and it became an unspoken command. Glasses, broken and whole, went flying everywhere, and yet somehow no one was hurt—we barely flinched. Here was an appropriate act of devastation, homage perhaps to the self-destruction that we'd all engaged in here.

And as the daylight shone through the cathartic cascade raining from the walls and ceiling, I realized this insanity was fitting for a place that had been home to so much, and so many. Even though the end of Freddy's was a brutal result of gentrification, we had been given a rare opportunity so often denied us for other disappearing corners of "old" New York. Drunk and wistful, and squinting at the rising sun through a shower of broken glass, we said a final, proper goodbye.

MARGARITA MEYENDORFF

Margarita Meyendorff (Mourka) is the author of the memoir, *DP: Displaced Person*. The daughter of a Russian baron, she was born displaced, far from the opulence of Imperial Russia that was her birthright. A series of wars destroyed this privileged existence, and Margarita's life became a series of extraordinary moves. She has performed as an actress, dancer, musician, and storyteller at venues throughout the United States and in Europe.

THE AFTER HOURS BAR

Margarita Meyendorff

New York City, 1969. They had fled the Old Country, and at eighteen, I fled them. I left my parents, the Baron and Baroness Meyendorff sitting, with their titles and their piles of paper, as dusty and outdated as they were, stuffed into a tiny apartment in the Russian expatriate enclave of Nyack. I was escaping to The Big Apple to make it as an actress. It wasn't long before I was out on the street—angry and broke.

With trepidation, I walk up three flights of stairs of a midtown Manhattan building, and open the door into a dingy, cluttered office. I am responding to an ad I saw in *Backstage*: "Go-Go Agent Looking for Girls." I step into the room and am surrounded by hundreds of black and white photos of dancing girls displaying their beautiful bodies in a multitude of poses and costumes.

Oh My God, I could never look like that. I begin to turn back when Phil, the dance agent, glances up, takes his feet off the desk and introduces himself. It is too late to run. Phil asks me to put on my costume and do some dance moves. My heart sinks. I don't have a costume yet, I tell him. No problem, just strip down to your underwear, he says. In spite of the initial embarrassment of having to dance in underwear that had seen better days, I close my eyes, and slink into a blues number I conjure up in my head. After about thirty seconds, Phil thanks me, hires me on the spot, lends me money for an outfit and gives me the address of my first gig. I am in. To hell with all nine to five secretarial jobs!

With my new black go-go outfit: bra, panties, fringe, fishnet stockings with the seam down the back and red high heels, I take the subway to my first job—an illegal after hours bar on West 19th—the warehouse district.

I ring the bell and soon hear the machinery of an elevator. A face appears in the porthole.

"Yeah?"

"It's Mourka. Mourka, the dancer!?"

A guy by the name of Jerry wearing a suit made out of some slippery silvery stuff, opens the door with a key. A few floors up—God knows how many—he opens up another door with a key. The whole place is wrapped in aluminum foil. Every single thing is glittery silver metal and mirrors. From the middle of the ceiling hangs a silver cage. Oh shit! Jerry leads me into a small dressing room and hands me a large round hatbox.

"Take that off and wrap yourself in this."

"Aluminum foil? I can't dance in aluminum foil."

"So? Dance different."

"Listen, I don't just bump and grind. I'm a jazz dancer. I ... dance. I can't dance in aluminum foil."

"Hey. This is what you gotta wear. We got a concept here."

"Get somebody else."

"What do you mean get somebody else? I got no time for this crap. Alright! Wear what you got, put this on over ... No? Jesus Christ. We'll add one hundred dollars to what we're paying you—Dese freakin' artist types."

So I'm dancing in this cage wrapped in aluminum foil. The cage is suspended several feet off the ground. It turns when I turn and swings when I move. I slide in my high heels. I have to hold onto the bars to stay vertical. Yards of foil are shivering and crackling around me. The music blares; the large crowd drinks, smokes weed, ogles, jeers.

At six o'clock in the morning, I take the subway home with two hundred and fifty dollars I have hidden in my shoes. Jerry asks me back the next night. I will make more money in two days than I made working a full week at my previous job. I feel rich.

When I tell my Russian baroness mother I'm dancing in bars, she says, "Wear a mask and nobody will know it is you."

INES RODRIGUES

Ines Rodrigues is a Brazilian journalist married to an Irishman, living in New York for over a decade. She attends courses and workshops at The Writing Institute at Sarah Lawrence College. Ines' first novel, *Days of Bossa Nova*, takes place in her hometown of São Paulo, and she recently read excerpts of it at the conference Journée du Monde in Paris, France. She published a short story at the website *The Good Book Corner* and wrote fiction and non-fiction for magazines, such as *Elle* and *Marie Claire*. She lived in London for four years before landing in Scarsdale, New York, where she currently teaches Italian, writes, raises her two children, and spoils their two cats.

THE PUB TEST

Ines Rodrigues

You don't marry an Irishman without passing the pub test. I'm Brazilian, but a life of Carnival didn't prepare me to step with ease into my future husband's bar culture. Many years ago, David moved to São Paulo on a work assignment. Soon he stood above the crowd: tall, white as paper, and keeping his feet always glued to the ground during our wild dancing parties. "You dance, I drink" he used to say. For a year I took him to sandy beaches and to the best steakhouses, where a carnivore like him almost cried of joy over cuts of meat so juicy they seemed to be alive. His most romantic line was "I like to spend time with you." It took me another year to get my seal of approval on my first trip to Ireland, but it had nothing to do with meeting the parents. I had to meet the pub.

I landed in cloudy Dublin on December 26th, after flying for fourteen hours from São Paulo. David opened his long arms to greet me at the arrivals hall and said: "I hope you are not tired, I want you to meet some friends."

I just had time to fake a smile and lie: "Of course not." My red eyes watched him throw my bags in the trunk and off we drove to a town with a castle called Malahide. His best friend Michael owned an old stone house that looked like a mini castle. Michael welcomed me with a hug, his rugby player body in contrast to childish gray eyes. He introduced me to twenty other friends who were all feasting on Christmas leftovers and Burgundy wine. I joined them and for the next two hours I ate, drank and answered questions, from Brazilian politics to bikinis. My bones felt like rubber when someone said: "Are we ready? Let's go?"

"Go where?" I asked David with wide eyes. Aren't we going to sleep here?"

"We are going to the pub," he said, pulling me by the hand.

We walked fast, the *tac tac* of our heels resonating across the street. The place had stonewalls, low ceilings with wood beams and a fireplace. Our large group stood at the bar and I ordered my first real Irish Guinness from a rosy-cheeked lady. Guinness in Ireland is creamier, less watery, round and richer. "It's the water," the Irish say. "It's mother's milk." David added. As I gulped my first pint, I forgot my squared bottom from sitting on the plane and the effort to understand the new accents. The second and third Guinness came along as I learned they always take turns, so one person buys a round of drinks for everyone at a time. They don't bother sitting because while standing they can speak louder, make better jokes and gesticulate like Italians. I lost track of time and pints, I was not completely plastered—a new word in my English vocabulary – when Michael started singing. His father, an older and shorter version of him, joined in "It's a Long Way to Tipperary" as they stood by the fireplace and the rest of the group clapped along. My future husband sat at the piano—I had no idea he was musical—and tapped a few notes. Other songs followed. Even the bar owner joined the chorus. The walk back home started at three in the morning under a cold drizzle. This time I couldn't hear the heels on the pavement, just the loud singing. I was arm-to-arm with the best friend's wife, and between wobbly steps and her silent complicity, I finally understood the Irish meaning of "I Do."

JOHN GREDLER

John Gredler, poet and memoirist, is a frequent contributor to 650 who's been writing in notebooks and journals for most of his adult life. He honed his craft at the Writing Institute at Sarah Lawrence College, Bella Villa Writers, 125, and the Terzo Piano Workshops. A recipient of the 2014 Kathryn Gurfein Fellowship from The Writing Institute at Sarah Lawrence College, John's work has been published in *Atticus Review, Fictionique, Narratively, Dan's Papers, Westchester Review,* and *Talking Writing.* John lives and writes in Tuckahoe, New York.

BEFORE THE FALL

John Gredler

The boy is in the locker room shower with his dad after a swim in the saltwater pool. He looks up at the man with wonder as he soaps up, water washing the suds off his back and down his long legs.

The father dries the boy and wraps a towel around him. Outside the showers they rinse their bathing suits in the big square sink and run them through the double-rolled ringer. The boy asks if he can turn the cast iron crank and the father says yes, helping him push it when it gets stuck.

They walk the gray-painted wood plank floor, the boy sliding his feet on the wet slippery spots, the father saying, "Be careful."

At their changing room, the father spins the black-numbered dial of the combination lock and it quickly opens. He pulls back the hasp and swings open the door. Inside it is not much bigger than a closet with a bench on one end and metal hooks on the unpainted walls holding towels and clothing. There is a single shelf high up with a thick unframed piece of mirror, one corner broken off, leaning at an angle against the wall. His father stands him on the bench and helps him dress telling him to step into his briefs.

After he is dressed, the boy leans back and watches his father as he combs his still wet hair in the mirror. When he is done, he takes a last look at his reflection and runs his thumbs over his eyebrows, smoothing them out. The father turns, "Ready?"

Up at the bar, the father sits the boy on a high stool and orders him a Shirley Temple. "No, I want a James Bond." The bartender laughs, "A James Bond it is."

His father orders a beer. It comes in an iced mug, the foamed head overflowing, dripping down the sides. The boy scratches at the layer of frost on the glass scraping in his initials before his father picks it up and takes a long pull. "That's good," he says as he puts the beer down on the bar.

The boy touches the foam with his finger, licks it and frowns at the pungent taste. He then sips his drink through a thin red straw. The super sweetness of the puddled cherry juice at the bottom of the glass erases the bitterness of the beer from his mouth. The father lights a cigarette and is laughing at something the bartender said. He drains his beer and orders another. The boy says, "Can we go outside?"

The father lifts the boy down from his stool and hands him his drink. They walk out the heavy glass-paneled, wood-framed doors to the wide veranda and walk across the varnished deck to the big rocking chairs coated with so many layers of thick dark green paint that the wicker has become a solid surface.

The boy climbs onto one of the chairs and looks at his drink. The maraschino cherry is still suspended on top of the pile of ice chips. He takes the plastic stir stick with the blue and white flag and the letters LYC impressed on it and spears the cherry.

Engulfed by the chair, he sits eating the cherry slowly. Looking out at the boats rocking in the harbor, he listens to the sounds of the wind blown stays snapping against aluminum masts and he watches the sailors, coming in off the launches, drop their sail bags on the sloping green lawn as they make their way up to the bar.

DAVID MASELLO

David Masello moved to New York more than thirty years ago from Evanston, Illinois, and he has made his living as a writer and editor ever since. He began his career as a nonfiction book editor at Simon & Schuster, then went on to hold senior editorial positions at many magazines, including *Travel & Leisure, Art and Antiques,* and *Town and Country,* where he was features editor. He's currently executive editor of *Milieu,* a magazine about design and architecture. He's a widely published essayist and poet, with pieces appearing in *The New York Times, Salon, Best American Essays,* and numerous literary and art magazines. His plays have been produced and performed by the Manhattan Repertory Theatre, Jewish Women's Theatre of Los Angeles, Big Apple Theatre Festival, and Fresh Fruit Festival. He is the author of two books about art and architecture.

TIME TO GO HOME

David Masello

When I was young and single, going to gay bars alone felt like a necessary duty—something to be endured for the betterment of the self. "Go now!" I would coach myself late on Saturday nights in my 11th Street tenement, knowing even then, as a twenty-something-year-old, that youth was a temporary state. "Stay here, watch another rerun of 'The Honeymooners' and you're guaranteed to remain single."

And, so, despite the allure of the bed, the mewings of cats in the courtyard below, and the comfort that came with reciting the banter between Ralph and Alice Kramden, I would dress the role and make my way to the bar of the moment. I might walk east a half-hour to Boy Bar on St. Mark's, where, ominously one night, seemingly overnight, the bartenders had donned elbow-length rubber gloves in response to an epidemic that seemed unstoppable, afraid even to put their bare fingers into the used glasses. I might go to Wildwood with its flannel-clad "clones," not my aesthetic, but at least I stood out; Uncle Charlie's in unsexy Murray Hill; The Web, with its

Colonial-era dynamic of younger Asians seeking older Caucasians; or the Ninth Circle in the Village, where its Dantesque basement was populated by rentboys while upstairs the hoi polloi and haughty alike gathered in a state of Hellish limbo (it was there, apocryphally, where Edward Albee found his title, "Who's Afraid of Virginia Woolf," scrawled on a restroom wall).

Wherever I wound up, I would leave by one or two in the morning, often haunted by the visage of a certain stranger in the crowd I hadn't the courage to approach. I would ponder on my train ride or walk back home the idea of placing one of those "I saw you, you looked at me" ads on the back page of the Village Voice—though the urge would usually, thankfully, abate by morning. But I was grateful, too, to be heading home alone on the subway with the Sunday Times on my lap, its weight and just-off-the-press warmth sufficient to evoke the presence of another person.

I no longer go to gay bars. I am in my fifties, hardly an asset in such places and I don't expect to be any more adept at negotiating bar protocol than I was in my twenties. When I look into the few bars that exist along Eighth Avenue or Christopher Street, as I pass them, I see many faces in the crowd lit by the screens of their phones, an easy method for pretending to be occupied by contact with others elsewhere and, thus, avoid the live bluntness of rejection now. We had no such props, apart from the lighting of a cigarette or fishing in a cocktail glass between ice cubes for the maraschino cherry.

Yet, I feel a certain nostalgia for the bars I used to visit because they were places where a young gay man could be surrounded by his peers, be actually shoulder to shoulder with them. One of the things you realize when you're older is that you were attractive as a young man, though you didn't know so at the time. Although the house odds of meeting someone never improved for me, there was always the lure of the jackpot—that potential for sex, a real boyfriend, a new friend. There was also the guarantee of disappointment and hurt—boredom, ego-deflating rejection, smoke-cured hair, the igniting of a randiness that felt lit by an eternal flame. Whether I felt welcomed in the places or shunned, flirted with or passed by, I had the privilege of age then; membership was a given.

I learned early on—and it is a lesson that has endured—that the secret strategy for going to gay bars is to know their limitations, when it's alright to go inside and socialize, and when it's time to leave and go home.

JOHN PIELMEIER

John Pielmeier began his career with the play and movie *Agnes of God*. Since then, he has had three more plays mounted on Broadway and twenty-five film, television movies and miniseries produced. Most recently he has written and acted in the internationally successful limited series, *The Pillars of the Earth*, and his stage adaptation of *The Exorcist* premiered in the West End in 2017 and is bound for Broadway. His first novel, *Hook's Tale*, was published by Scribner in July 2017. In between, he has received the Humanitas Award (plus two nominations), five Writers' Guild Award nominations, a Gemini Award (plus a nomination), an Edgar Award, the Camie Award, a Christopher Award, and been nominated for the Emmy Award (three times) and the Golden Globe Award. He is married to writer Irene O'Garden and makes his home in upstate New York.

NINE DOGS WAITING TO PEE

John Pielmeier

If you walked down the basement stairs of my Aunt Evelyn and Uncle Ott's house and turned right past the tool cave, you'd step into a room of enchantment.

Its dimensions were twenty by thirty, maybe, and it was windowless. On the wall to the right was a framed question: What baseball score do these pictures illustrate? Below was a triptych depicting 1) a bottle of scotch emptying its final drop, 2) a bare-breasted lady, and 3) a toilet. You lifted up a piece of paper for the answer: Last of the Fifth, Two Out, Nobody On.

Twelve-year-old Me found this clever. Besides, it was the only time I was allowed to look at a pair of naked boobies without my mother pulling me away. I could look at them again and again. I could ponder.

At the far end of the room stood a little bar with lots of glasses Uncle Ott called highballs.

Above was a photo of Evelyn and Ott standing on a deck of a cruise ship embarking for Bermuda with all of Evelyn's rich widowed friends.

Nearby was a glass painting of a waterfall and if you plugged it in, something behind the glass would turn and the waterfall would look almost real.

There was a button that you were to push if you had any complaints, except it had a little hole in its center, and when you pushed it a needle came out and stuck you in the finger.

Best of all there were two nickel slot-machines.

My sister and I would ask Ott for nickels whenever we visited, which as a family was only on Thanksgiving. Ott was bald, fat and jolly and would sing "I'm Forever Blowing Bubbles" in a beautiful tenor voice but Evelyn was distant. Thanksgiving consisted of their grown children - my older cousins - and their grandchildren and us. I was in-between. I had to play with the youngers in the bar while the grown-ups had highballs upstairs and laughed. After turkey, I got into political discussions with my older cousin Joe who was conservative and made me feel stupid and angry. Once my younger cousin Chris punched me in the stomach. I never fit in.

Like the bar. The house was tidy and tasteful. Not the bar.

It had a painting of nine dogs standing upright waiting to pee on a fire hydrant.

It had a painting of six dogs playing poker.

It had a little mechanical hobo that if you pushed a button would dance and hold out his hat for a tip, and another with a doctor who would drink from a bottle and then pretend to operate on someone, his nose glowing red behind the surgical mask.

When I was in high school, Aunt Evelyn had an operation that removed part of her brain. She was never sure who I was after that, but she

46

was nicer.

None of her rich widowed friends came to visit.

There were no more Thanksgivings.

One January, rewiring something under the sink, Ott electrocuted himself. Evelyn went into a nursing home, and whatever mind she had left sailed to Bermuda. The house was turned into apartments and sold.

I never visited the bar again.

A few years ago, on a trip back to my hometown, I went to pick up a peach pie from a lady who baked them in her home. It was Evelyn and Ott's home, and when I told her who I was, she invited me inside.

She and her husband had lovingly restored the house. It was tidy and tasteful and when I asked her if the bar was still in the basement she smiled and said yes, it was.

This made me happy, as happy as Last of the Fifth, Two Out, Nobody On.

As happy as if I had just had a highball.

EDWARD McCANN

650 founder and editor **Edward McCann** is a writer whose features and essays have been published in national magazines and literary journals such as *Better Homes & Gardens, Country Living, Good Housekeeping, Milieu, the Sun,* the *Irish Echo* and others. An award-winning television writer/producer and longtime contributing editor at *Country Living,* Ed is a member of New York City-based Artists Without Walls and Irish American Writers & Artists. He's recently completed a memoir about the search for his missing nephew, and his essay, "Pregnant Again," was selected for the anthology, *Listen To Your Mother,* published by Penguin Books in April, 2015. He lives and writes in New York's Hudson River Valley.

ACKNOWLEDGMENTS

We thank Nancy Manocherian's the cell, which supported Read650 at its inception. A twenty-first century salon in the heart of New York City, their mission is to support the arts and incubate new works, and the cell made its beautiful performance space available to Read650 as we were finding our way. The cell: To mine the mind, pierce the heart, and awaken the soul.
TheCellTheatre.org

Artists Without Walls was created to inspire, uplift, and unite people and communities of diverse cultures through the pursuit of artistic achievement, and has supported and encouraged Read650 from its beginnings. Artists Without Walls: No Limits. No Walls. No Boundaries.
ArtistsWithoutWalls.com

We're grateful for the support and encouragement from The Writing Institute at Sarah Lawrence College, which supplies a steady stream of excellent writers to Read650. The Writing Institute helps writers in all genres progress and grow in their craft and welcomes them all into a very supportive community.
SarahLawrence.edu

READ650.COM

INFO @READ650.COM
FACEBOOK.COM/READ650